# The Power of Laughter:
## Managing Change with a Sense of Humor

Copyright © 2018 by Carla M. Rieger. All rights reserved. No part of this book may be reprinted or reproduced, or utilized in any form by electronic, mechanical or other means now known or invented in the future without express written consent of the author.

Printed in Canada
ISBN # 978-1-9858881-0-4

Anand Publishing educational products are available at special discount for bulk purchases of 10 or more.

Anand Publishing<br>
#138 – 2912 W. Broadway,<br>
Vancouver, B.C.<br>
CANADA V6K 0E9<br>
Tel: (604) 222-2276

Written, researched and compiled
by
Carla Rieger


Edited
by
Ron Adams

# Table of Contents

Introduction: Tales of a Reformed Curmudgeon     5

Chapter 1:   How Laughter Makes You Smarter     8
Chapter 2:   How to Marry Work and Play     11
Chapter 3:   How Play Activates an Adventurous Spirit     14
Chapter 4:   How to Use Joy to Trigger Forgiveness     19
Chapter 5:   How to Heal the Playful Self     21
Chapter 6:   Mindset & Your Health     27
Chapter 7:   How to Take the Humor Risk     31
Chapter 8:   Types of Humor to Use at Work     35
Chapter 9:   Fun at Work Ideas     40
Chapter 10:  6 Mistakes to Avoid     46
Chapter 11:  Discover Your Humor Personality Style     48
Chapter 12:  Reclaiming Your Birthright to Live Joyfully     73

About the Author     76

# Introduction
## Tales of a Reformed Curmudgeon

*While it may be love that makes the world go round it is laughter that keeps us from getting dizzy.*

I call myself a reformed curmudgeon. I was born into a family that had AADS – Acquired Amusement Deficiency Syndrome. They were academic, serious, hard-working immigrants who not only didn't have time for humor, they didn't even get it. Jokes flew over the tops of their heads several times a day.

I remember as a child I heard a joke at school, so that same night at the dinner table I said,

"Mom, why don't cannibals like to eat clowns?"

"I haven't the slightest idea," my mother replied in her upper class British accent.

I offer the famous punch line, "Because they taste funny!"

My mother replied, straight-faced, "That doesn't make any sense, dear. Clowns aren't known to frequent the jungles of Africa where cannibals would be found. Eat your beans now and be quiet."

So, after a while I stopped "wasting my time" on the frivolities of humor. Instead I followed in both my parents' footsteps and became very serious and achievement-oriented. And after seven years of post-secondary education while working two jobs, something snapped.

I was taking a leadership program and I was standing on a stage in front of 65 people talking about my project. Finally, the leader of the program, who was an acting coach from the Bronx, stopped me.

She asked, "How old are you?"

"I'm 23. Why do you ask?"

"Because you act like a 45 year old insurance underwriter."

The rest of the class erupted into laughter. Many heads were nodding.

"Why do you say that?

"Because you are so serious. You're only 23. You should lighten up. Life is too important to be taken seriously. If you're this dull and serious now what are you going to be like in 20 years? Now get off the stage and come back when you've learned how to lighten up."

I remember driving home that day thinking, *maybe she is right. Maybe I am overly serious.* I'd wake up every morning and go for a five mile run, pump iron, then eat my quarter cup of low-fat yogurt and my one celery stick. My wardrobe consisted of colors such as taupe, charcoal and pewter. My idea of fun was reading my calculus text book and cleaning the bathroom tiles with a toothbrush.

That experience actually scared me enough to make some changes. A friend of mine was taking a comedy improvisation class, so I signed up. I was terrible at first, but they forced me to get up over and over again. I saw that I survived the humiliation of failure. Bit by bit I got better. I started to actually like it. After that I jumped into anything comedy related---sketch comedy, stand-up, comedy writing, clowning and cartooning. I worked HARD at comedy, because that was my style. Luckily however, after a while, the real essence of laughter started to permeate my soul. I mellowed out, and developed a much more fun-loving, celebratory, light-hearted personality.

And now that I'm pushing 45 (and I'm not saying from which side), I've noticed a few things. I'm far less anxious and more relaxed. I'm less boring and more interesting. I'm less cynical and more hopeful. I'm less self-critical and more confident. I dress more colorfully and, quite frankly, I'm more popular. There is an old saying that goes, "Lighten up and your network will grow, because people will be attracted by the light."

There was another event that had a huge impact on this change in my personality and on the career I chose, which I'll tell you about a bit later on in this book. All this to say, I realized that everyone has a sense of humor – it's just that some of us forget to use it. It's like a piece of software that's been bundled with our hard drives. I just knew that if a killjoy like me could lighten, I figured anyone could, so I got on a mission.

# Chapter 1
## How Laughing Makes Your Smarter

*At the height of laughter the universe is flung into a
kaleidoscope of new possibilities.*
Jean Houston, Behavioral Scientist

Candace Pert, in her bestselling book *Molecules of Emotion*, says that your frontal cortex allows you to choose what to pay attention to. At any given moment there is so many stimuli going on that you can't focus on all of it. As a result, the brain has evolved to the point where we can choose what to consciously pay attention to. If you focus on what you love, what you enjoy, what you are grateful for - the pleasure hormones increase. This in turn nourishes your organs and your whole physiology profoundly.

We are in an evolutionary process. Early humans used the inner core of the brain stem, known as the reptilian brain, to survive. Over the millenniums we started developing more layers to the brain as a method for dealing with external reality. For example, the neocortex is like the most advanced part of our bio-computer, whereby you have access to much more advanced "brain software".

However, we still revert to the survival brain in certain "triggering" situations. If someone cuts you off in traffic, or speaks to you in a certain tone of voice, the energy will leave the neocortex and center around the survival brain again. Those times when you act "reactive" can often feel embarrassing once your neocortex switches on again.

When you laugh, it activates more of your whole brain and can instantly release you from a "triggered" state of mind.

It allows for greater breathing and relaxation. In fact, you can't hold your breath and laugh at the same time. Think of the last time you found something very funny. Try to imagine yourself holding your breath and laughing. It's impossible, right? This opens up whole brain thinking again and then you become aware of a wider array of responses. In short, it brings forth you "better self".

While there is increasing amounts of data to back up the benefits of laughter and play, there is anecdotal evidence as well. A survey appeared in *Marriage Magazine* that interviewed 100 couples married for 20 years or more who considered their marriage to be very successful. They were asked to list the top 10 qualities that went into making their marriage successful. Almost across the board the couples listed "the ability to play, laugh and have fun with my partner" within the top three qualities. Most people listed sex as number eight or nine. It just goes to show that improving your *laugh life* may be even more important that improving your sex life.

Research conducted by psychologist Ashton Trice at Mary Baldwin College in Virginia showed that humor helps us think. Trice's research showed that taking time out to laugh can help us to get rid of negative feelings and allow us to return to a task. As you will see in the chapter on *Embarrassing Incidents*, laughter can help you let go and move on to another project, unaffected by past defeat.

Laughter releases endorphins, a chemical 10 times more powerful than the pain-relieving drug morphine. It can offer the same exhilarating effect as doing strenuous exercise.

A survey by Hodge-Cronin & Associates found that of 737 CEOs surveyed, 98 percent preferred job candidates with a sense of humor. Another survey indicated that 84 percent of the executives thought that employees with a sense of humor do a better job than people with little or no sense of humor.

Dr. David Abramis at California State Long Beach has studied having fun at work for years. He discovered that people who have fun on the job are more creative, more productive, better decision-makers and get along better with co-workers. They also have fewer absentee and sick days than people who aren't having fun.

# Chapter 2
## How to Marry Work and Play

Even though I had encountered both empirical and anecdotal evidence to prove that fun at work was important, it was hard for me to believe. When I first joined the workforce in my 20's, I was very serious, hardworking and diligent.  I thought this was what the workplace wanted of me.  The "Protestant Work Ethic" program had been passed down through my bloodline for centuries. Not to mention that my work environments totally validated my all-work, no-play ethic. Those who cracked a smile were reprimanded.

That all changed in 1988 when I got a new job with a teambuilding firm.  The company was called Playfair. The job involved training people how to create a playful community on college campuses and in workplaces.

They invited me to California for my first Company retreat. My first clue that this was a "different" kind of company was when I was told that the person picking me up at the airport was the "Senior Vice Emperor." I asked how I could recognize him. He said "Oh, YOU'LL recognize me." When I arrived at the airport there was a sea of people, but one man did indeed stood apart from the rest of the crowd because he was wearing a gigantic fish on his head -- a ball cap with a fish head out the front and a fish tail out the back.

Once inside the office, I was invited to wear pink bunny eared slippers. In the front hall I walked under a banner that said "The company that plays together stays together." At the time I didn't realize how true that would be.

We entered the Vice Emperor's office and it was like going into a section of Toys-R-Us. There were fuzzy dice, a game of checkers, mobiles hanging from the ceiling. One section of the room was referred to as the stress management centre, and there stood a 4-foot blow up clown and huge boxing mits. Anytime anyone wanted to let off some steam they could just take a few punches at the clown. I was offered the gloves to relieve my travel stress. I took one hit. He flew to the ground and then bounced right back up smiling again.

The Vice Emperor ushered me into the waiting room to wait for the other new arrivals. I thought I'd help myself to some nuts in a can on the table. As soon as I opened the can a spring-loaded snake projectiled out.

I was starting to get nervous. My usual way of getting validation was displaying my serious, no nonsense, work ethic. Now that seemed like a liability in this company. I thought it was just a matter of time before they replaced me.

I made it through first re-treat which was wildly playful from morning until night AND we still got lots of work done. They certainly proved to be a company that had successfully married work and play.

My job was to now go out and make campuses and workplaces more playful. It was hard at first. At that time, fun at work was a very new concept and people viewed you as flakey at best and a downright liability to the organization at worst.

Over time, however, we were able to prove that a fun working environment meant bosses were more likely to keep good people, even if they weren't paying top dollar. It seemed to lower turnover and absenteeism. People gladly worked overtime when necessary because they felt like they were part of a fun community—they cared more about their job. They had bonded through fun and therefore felt a responsibility to help each other throughout the workday. And the best part was that they got their work done without feeling so exhausted at the end of the day.

Today, I don't work for that company anymore, but I'm still very bonded to all the people I worked with back then. Many of the original members 40 years later are still working together. The front hall banner was indeed correct – the company that plays together stays together.

# Chapter 3
## How Play Activates an Adventurous Spirit

I think you can tell a lot about how people handle stress and change by how they ride a roller coaster. Think of that last time you went on a ride like that. There is a spectrum of roller coaster riding behavior, and it's important to identify where you are on that continuum. In my early years, I found myself completely on one side of that spectrum. I avoid that ride whenever possible. On one occasion, a fiendish friend talked me into it. I sat in the middle car, figuring it would be the safest. I held onto the handlebar for dear life and squeezed my eyes shut the entire ride, praying for the moment it would end. Then I ran to the bathroom to throw up. And, I vowed to myself never to ride again.

On the other end of the continuum are the people I used to envy. These are the people who run for the front car of the roller coaster. They sit back, arms draped along the back of the seat, looking totally relaxed. As soon as the roller coaster has climbed to the top of the first hill, what do these people usually do? They throw both hands in the air, and scream and laugh as they race down the track. They let go and let the ride take them. As soon as the ride is over they usually want to go again, right?

I had often wondered what it would take to be like that. One day I found out. It was one simple thing. I had just presented at a huge business conference in San Diego. I was sitting in the lounge with some colleagues and we noticed a roller coaster across the street. Soon they all wanted to go and I politely declined.

"I don't like roller coasters," I told them. "I have a kind of phobia."

One of them said, "But you just gave a presentation on change!"

I defended myself, "That's got nothing to do with roller coasters."

They convince me that it does indeed, and they encouraged me to join them. On the walk over there, they tell me the one thing that makes all the difference. Can you guess what it is?

One of my friends says, "Throw your hands in the air. Open your eyes. Breath. Just let go and let the ride take you. Don't fight it."

I said, "I'm not going to do that! I'll be sucked out and fall forty feet to my death."

"Thousands of people do it every day. Trust us."

They buy me a ticket and put me in line for the front car. I stand next to the height meter in hopes of getting out of it that way. Unfortunately, I'm a foot taller than the minimum height requirement. I get in line and my friends leave me there. They go buy corn dogs, grab a bench next to the roller coaster so they can watch.

Meanwhile I'm standing there along with all the 12-year-olds wearing my blue, corporate pant suit, waiting for my turn. I see people in front get in the cars. Two minutes later I hear blood curdling screams. Finally the car pulls up again and I am sure a couple of people are missing.

Finally, my turn comes. I settle into the front car and the attendant buckles me in with a seat belt that looks like it's been there since 1953. The handlebar is a flimsy piece of aluminum. It certainly doesn't look up to Consumer Product Safety Standards. I remember reading that roller coasters generally accelerate from 0 to 82 mph in 2.3 seconds. These kinds of G-forces aren't even experienced by fighter pilots who are equipped with full body safety harness, crash helmet AND a parachute. We have none of this.

The ride lurches forward and we are on our way. We roll past my gang who are giving me the thumbs up and reminding me to let go. I'm trying not to white knuckle the handlebar. My heart starts beating faster, my palms are sweating, and my breathing gets shallow. The ride starts to inch its way up the first hill. I hear the rattling of a very old suspension system. The higher we get to the top, the more I see the fairgrounds take shape below me; little people safely on the ground, the sun setting in the distance. I take in a deep breath trying oh so hard to just enjoy the view. Until, of course, we get to the top of the first hill.

It stays there for a few moments before hurtling down the track. I'm forcing myself to lift my hands in the air until I hear the girl behind me scream "Oh…………..my………….god!"

I instead wrap myself around the handlebar and squeeze my eyes shut. I resist the downward motion with every cell in my body until I feel nauseous.

As soon as the ride comes up the next hill, I open one eye and I see the setting sun off in the distance. I remember my commitment to let go. I take in a deep breath and release my grip. I throw my arms up in the air, open my eyes, breathe and let the ride take me. The ride goes thundering down the track again and the g-force pulls me to a standing position. Tears are streaming out of my eyes. I scream so loud that only dolphins can probably hear me. However, once down the second hill I'm starting to laugh because I realize I let go and survived!

I laugh the whole rest of the ride. And as soon as the ride is over -- guess what? I didn't need to throw up. No motion sickness. Strange. Instead, I'm exhilarated. I decide I need to go again and I go two more times. And I didn't feel nauseous at all. After that it miraculously cured me of car sickness, air sickness and sea sickness, too.

Roller coasters are indeed a great metaphor for change. There are times in life when the roller coaster is going up – good income, good health, your car passes the emissions test… whatever. But eventually it starts to go down again. Maybe you have a financial downturn, or a health issue, or a relationship breakup, or just a bad mood.

When you're moving up the hill, you tend to have a large perspective on the world. You may feel tolerant, light-hearted and creative. From this perspective you can easily see another person's point of view. When things go wrong, you can laugh and try something new. People enjoy your presence. Life just flows.

During the downward process, however, things can change—just like the seasons. Summer becomes fall and fall becomes winter. You head down to the bottom trenches of the roller coaster. Down there things seem dark and chaotic. Life seems hard and frustrating. All your problems appear larger than life. Other people can really irritate you. What was once cute is now grounds for legal action. You are petty.

The good news is, you don't stay down there either. Life shifts again. You come back up the hill. You get that perspective back. You find yourself apologizing to people for being so cranky. You can't understand what came over you. A sigh of relief fills you as the landscape below takes shape again. But not for long, because down you go again!

It's the nature of being human. These changes are easier to see in others, of course. Especially the people you live with. However, you go through them, too. And if you look back over your life most people tend to agree that life is like a roller coaster.

The truth is, if it's been a roller coaster for most of your life, chances are it's going to continue to be a roller coaster until the day you die. You can ride the roller coaster of life holding on, contracting, trying to deny those ups and downs and making yourself miserable and sick. Alternatively, you can let go, open your eyes, lean into the ride and laugh the whole way.

"I can't cover the mortgage payment this month! Woo-hoo! Here we go! Five people are sick today at work and I'm covering for everyone! Yee-hahh!!!

The late, great father of modern psychology, Dr. Carl Jung, said we all have a variety of archetypal energy patterns in our psyche. We have such characters as the magician, the child, the warrior, the hero, the jester, the king, the queen, the beggar, the sage, and on and on. The jester or the fool is the part of every human that can let go and step off the edge and just trust that life will provide. Therefore, the next time life is taking a downward turn, see if you can access that inner jester so you can let go and laugh. You will be amazed at how much more exciting life can be.

If you tend to dislike change or overly try to control things in life to the point of making yourself and others miserable, my challenge to you is to go on a roller coaster – hands free. If you've never done that before, see how it feels. It will give you the kind of physical, kinesthetic experience needed to help you bring that attitude into the rest of your life.

# Chapter 4
## How to Use Joy to Trigger Forgiveness

Joy can transform us from having a narrow perspective, a clenched heart, or even bitterness. We've all probably worked with or lived with people who have "rubbed us the wrong way." Over the years the little things that don't get resolved build up into walls. It's easy to become a Scrooge to some people, because of that thing they did years ago, not willing to warm your heart to them anymore.

One experience that helped me choose joy over bitterness was simply watching the film *Immortal Beloved*. It's about the life of Beethoven. Beethoven wrote the music "Ode to Joy" which is one of his most brilliant pieces. But, ironically he was the quintessential curmudgeon.

He had been very physically abused as a child and he was a very sensitive person. Anybody who crossed him in the wrong way was a target for his venom. There was a great scene in the end of the movie when he is conducting his last symphony. It was one of his most famous, the 9$^{th}$ symphony, which includes "Ode to Joy." There he is, a little, old, gnarly man, totally deaf. His sister-in-law comes to see the concert despite her hatred towards him. He had been cruel to her many ways over the years. He took away her son, called her names and ruined her family, but she had heard many favorable words about his latest symphony.

In the movie they depict his inspiration, his memories, for writing the different pieces of music. The memory from when he wrote "Ode to Joy" is when he was a boy. His father would come up to his bedroom in the middle of the night after a drinking binge and beat him. One night he hears his father coming up the stairs and he decides he is not going to let that happen this time. He climbs out his bedroom window, onto the roof and escapes to the street. He runs through the forest. He finds a beautiful lake in the middle of the forest, takes off his night shirt and swims into the middle. Then he floats on his back while looking at the stars. It is this moment he looks up at all the billions of stars on this spectacular summer night and feels safe once again and in awe of the glory that is.

As his sister-in-law is sitting there listening to Ode to Joy, tears are rolling down her cheeks. She narrates, "I listened to that music and all the hatred, bitterness and hurt that I had felt towards Beethoven just totally melted away. I just couldn't hate somebody who could write music like that."

That was such a powerful moment in the film. And when you think about it, joy can do that for people. Joy can melt away feels of hurt and anger and can bring you back to who you really are. It also lets you see others for who they really are. Any little moment that you can bring joy to people is great. I challenge you to find somebody who is locked away in a dark place. Take the risk of bringing a little joy to them and see what that feels like. The Dalai Lama once said, "Smile at the person who seems the unkind because they need it most."

# Chapter 5
## How to Heal the Playful Self

I'll tell you about someone I knew who did that for me.

My mother told me I never smiled for the first six years of my life. No one in my family really smiled much. Photos seem to prove that theory. I'm either scowling or pouting in every shot. My parents both worked most of the time and I was often left with overstressed neighbors or indifferent babysitters.

Something changed when I was seven years old, however, and my family joined some other families from our church, The Unitarian Church, to form a makeshift extended family. The Unitarian Church included people from many faiths and many philosophies. It attracted people who wanted community without too much dogma. In this extended family, there were about 28 of us. Every generation was represented. There were about six children from the ages of 7 to 11. I was the youngest.

In the beginning I disliked this community of people. I was seen as high maintenance and temperamental. People drew a wide berth around me, so I responded in kind. During the first few events I sat by myself while everyone else chatted and had fun. However, on one occasion a new member showed up. He was an older gentleman in his sixties, jolly, slightly rotund with white hair and a white beard. His name was Ted, and we ended up calling him Uncle Teddy.

One of the women in the group was organizing a Christmas event at the church. She took one look at Ted and convinced him to play Santa Claus at the Christmas service. This simply involved giving out little gifts to church members during the service. He valiantly accepted, but announced he had a bad hip and would need an elf to help deliver the gifts to audience members. At that point he leaned down and smiled at the children in the group.

All of them leapt to their feet and cried out "Pick me!"

"Now, have a seat. I'll have to see", said Ted.
Then he asked the hostess, "Are these ALL the children in the family group?"
She said, "I think the only one missing is Carla."
I was sitting on the staircase just outside the room.
"Come in here, Carla," Ted said in a sweet voice.

I didn't move at first. He was an adult, and I didn't trust adults. It was destined to be a bad experience. I wouldn't make a very good elf anyway. I'd have to wear a stupid costume. I t would be a lot of work. All in all, not for me.

I heard them carry on without me. I sat there grimly until a transformational thought occurred to me. What if he hadn't heard about my "difficult" reputation yet? I shyly crept into the room and sat behind the other children. The mother of the oldest child, Johnny, said that it would be best to choose her son since he was the most mature. My mother exclaimed how incredibly helpful and cooperative my older sister was. Another adult thought that Suzy, a year older than me, was the cutest.

Ted looked at us all, and then said, "I think I need Carla to be my elf".

There was a stunned silence, followed by a few gasps.

I heard someone whisper "I don't think you want to do that."

Ted was firm, though, and started talking immediately to the organizer about getting an elf costume for me.

The big day came and my mother warned me, "Don't make a fuss and ruin everything."

Ted took me aside and said, "Now I've seen in you an elf. All you have to do is let that elf come out and play. Okay?"

I rolled my eyes. Who wants to be a stupid elf?

The lady organizing the event is helping me into my costume. I put on the green frock with the jagged hem, the big brown belt, the pointy, felt hat, the striped stockings and saddle shoes with baubles on top. I look in the mirror and see an elf. It's not me.

I go backstage and Ted is fixing his red hat in the mirror. He glows and twinkles like a good Santa Claus should. I catch our reflection in a mirror. We looked magical. Uncle Teddy takes my hand and we enter the stage. The lights are bright, but I can just make out a sea of faces all waiting expectantly. Uncle Teddy begins ho-ho-hoing and slapping his belly. I just stand there staring into the lights. Santa opens his sack of gifts and holds up the first one while calling out a name.

"May Williamson!"

A lady in her eighties raises her hand. Santa hands the gift to me. I just stand there. He shooes me into the audience.

I shadow my eyes and see Mrs. Williamson. I walk over and hand her the gift. Her face beams. I glare back at her.

"Peter Johnston!"

I run back to the stage as fast as I can, and everyone laughs. I think they are laughing AT me, until I turn around and see warm, appreciative faces. I see Mr. Johnston's hand and I trot down to him.

He says, "You're a cute little elf."

I curtsy. More laughter. I see the delight in people's face and it started to thaw something in me. I become bolder. I run back up to Santa for my next assignment.

"Robbie Jamieson!"

That was the boy I secretly had a crush on. I run over to Robbie, give him the gift and kiss his cheek. We both blush. When I deliver a gift to Mr. Carruthers, he tips his hat.

When I give the Sunday school teacher, Mrs. Anderson, her gift she whispers, "Do your pirouette!"

I had been learning pirouettes in my ballet class. Mrs. Anderson caught me one day and complimented me on my ability. I run back to Santa and grab the gift for Janie Richards, my rival. She is sitting in the front row glaring at me. She wanted to be the Elf more than anything. I do a few pirouettes on my way to Janie. The audience bursts in spontaneous applause.

I am now on a roll. A few gifts later I try a running jeté down the center aisle. I finish the last gift with a couple of skillfully executed cartwheels landing with arms triumphant like an Olympic gymnast. Santa and I bow to a standing ovation.

We go backstage and several people from the extended family came back with us. They comment on how delightful I was, and how much they enjoyed our gift giving ceremony. My mother pushes through the crowd and announces, "You should wear that Elf costume more often!"

After that people in the group began to treat me differently. The adults saw the delightful side of me, and so did the other children. They included me and treated me as if I was wonderful to be around – and so I was. I no longer was the problem child, but instead a much happier one. I really appreciated Ted for that small gesture. He's passed away now, and probably never fully realized what a big difference that made for me.

Every year after that until I was 11, I was the Christmas elf with Uncle Teddy. We were a great team; everyone knew I was the elf and my role was never challenged. When I did finally give up my elf costume it was to a new, unhappy 7 year-old who needed to find her inner Elf.

Did anyone ever do that for you?
They saw a positive quality in you and helped you bring it out?

It's a very powerful thing to do for someone. Have you ever done it for anyone else? It may seem like a small gesture at the time, but it can have a very powerful and long-standing effect on someone.

Find someone over the next week that needs help getting back to who they really are. You can help them do that with a smile, a joke, including them in something fun, a gift like a helium balloon or an opportunity to go play. It can be a small or large gesture, but it's important to choose someone in a negative state of mind.

If you have a person in mind and you're afraid of getting your head bitten off, don't worry. If your act of joy gets rejected, above all, don't take it personally. The person just isn't ready or you need to try a more gentle approach. Regardless, if your intention is good, it will affect them in a positive way. It will start to melt their wall. Keep going until you find someone who accepts your gift.

# Chapter 6
## Mindsets & Your Health

Lack of joy can deeply affect your health. About 11 years ago I had allergies that wouldn't go away. I kept breaking out in hives. I couldn't link it to any type of food, because it was never consistent. I went to several doctors, and got no results. I tried alternative medicine such as acupuncture, herbal medicine, etc. Nothing worked. Then one day a friend told me about fasting.

> She said, "I tried juice fasting for a week - and I've never had hives since."
> I said, "Okay, I've tried everything else. I might as well give it a try."

I read a book that said you should always test your PH balance before you fast. If your system isn't alkaline enough, fasting could be dangerous. I get the PH testing papers. I test my saliva in the morning after drinking lemon juice - and I passed. I decide to wait a few days until the long weekend.

Over those few days I test myself each morning and each time I pass the test. But, on the day before I am to start fasting, I have a fight with my husband. It was one of those fights you have over little things, that aren't really about the little things -- like the garbage lid not being put back on tight enough so that the raccoons couldn't get in. It was really about both of us feeling overworked and there not being enough fun in our lives. Someone was responsible for the fact that one of us was going to have to clean up strewn garbage all over the back alley in the pouring rain.

And, of course, he was late for his flight out of town, so off he goes. And here I am, out in the alley, in the rain, in my nice outfit, picking up egg shells, old cartons and spaghetti. Leaves are blowing in my face. I'm running late for my meeting. And it really was him who didn't put the lid on the garbage can… really. I stew about this for the rest of the day, feeling angry, upset, irritated, hurt, going over the argument again and again in my mind. Have you ever done that?

The next morning when I test my PH, I am totally acidic. I read the book on fasting, and there is a whole chapter on how negative emotions can acidify your system. Perhaps it's where such expressions as "he's so bitter" or "she has a sweet disposition" come from. I was totally amazed. I wouldn't have believed it unless I'd seen it with my own eyes. I hadn't consumed anything differently. I had been in a negative state of mind all day.

I call my husband long distance and I say "Look we have to sort this thing out, I have to fast."

We heard each other out on our points of view, validated each other, and apologized for our behavior. We then joked about it and decided that raccoons are now just tricky experts in opening garbage can lids by themselves - so no one was to blame. We said *I love you*, to each other and we hung up. I felt much better, but it still took two more days for my system to become alkaline again.

Upon further research I discovered that emotions such as joy, laughter, fun, smiling, love, appreciation, gratitude, kindness all help the body become more alkaline. Since living in the modern world is a very acidifying experience, the more you can counteract it with alkaline foods and emotions, the more balanced your system will be.

In short, too much stress and negativity makes your:

- brain capacity decrease
- immune system go down
- circulation constrict
- breathing get shallow
- muscles tense
- digestion get worse
- mind close down
- level of distrust go up
- productivity decrease

Whereas, positive emotions make you

- brain capacity increase
- immune system go up
- circulation improve
- breathing get deeper
- muscles relax
- digestion get better
- mind become open to new possibilities
- level of trust go up
- productivity increase

This understanding along with fasting made the allergies disappear. Ever since then, anytime a negative event happens in my life, I don't so easily go into a reactive state. For example, I'm driving through traffic and another driver cuts me off. Part of me wants to curse, and another part of me says something like, "My health is more important than trying to righteously force that person to admit to he is a bad driver." Life is too short to spend it being self-righteous. It has helped me make that small choice over and over again. I've noticed these little drops in the bucket have created a large wellspring of greater peace of mind.

# Chapter 7
## How to Take the Humor Risk

*Laughter is the shortest distance between two people.*

One of the great things I created to help my inner curmudgeon is what I call a "Fun First Aid Kit." I have one in my car. Driving in heavy traffic can easily make me grouchy. Inside the kit is fun stuff. For example, I get to the bank, there is big long line. I'm a very impatient person by nature and I don't like lines, so, I read my **Far Side** cartoon book.

I remember doing this once. There I am in the bank. There is one teller. She is new and being trained. There was a big, long line, everybody is fuming and I'm the only one having a good time. I get up to the teller and she says, "You're the only one that's smiled at me."

Other things in my Fun First Aid Kit are bubbles and a fake cell phone. One day I went to the top of a big skyscraper and walked through the hallways one by one blowing bubbles. Then I got into the elevator to go down. There was a lawyer there on his cell phone talking away. After hearing his entire conversation down to floor 14, he got off the phone. At that point I pushed the ringer on my fake phone to make it ring. I said, "Hello." I listened for a moment, then looked over at the lawyer and handed him the phone. "It's for you."

One thing I used to enjoy doing was inviting friends or colleagues for a "pick your nose" lunch. You can tell who your friends are by whether they are willing to come with you. Then when they come to the restaurant they have to pick a nose that they are going to wear. They can be the clown, or the elephant, or they can be the Groucho, and they have to wear it the entire lunch. You get really excellent service when you wear stuff like this in a restaurant.

One time I went to lunch with a group of girlfriends and one of my friends had just broken up with someone. She was in a bad mood but I insisted she wear the nose. It's really hard to complain and be negative when you are wearing a clown nose. She started laughing instead.

In fact, there were two guys at another table and one of the guys had just said to his friend, "You know, I just want to meet a woman with a sense of humor."

His friend said "Look over there. There's four of them. Let's go talk to them."

For some reason, when you wear silly noses, people are more willing to talk to you and meet you. It is an ice breaker. They sat down with us and we joked around. By the end of the lunch, my friend ended up giving her number to the guy looking for a woman with a sense of humor! I felt personally responsible for starting that.

I'm the first to admit that taking that humor risk can be scary. I have been places where I want to lighten things up and it just doesn't work, or I can't find the courage. Having friends with you or a supporter is really helpful. For example, I was picking up somebody from the airport and she didn't know what I looked like. I decided that I would wear a big chicken mask. I emailed her beforehand, "Just look for the chicken." I thought it would be really funny until I got there and realized that I'd be the only one in the entire airport wearing a chicken mask, and I decided not to do it.

Then I ran into somebody I knew and told him that I was meeting somebody and I was going to wear the chicken mask but at that moment I was "chickening" out. He badgered me until I did it.

The minute I put it on people immediately started moving away from me, except for kids and old people. I made several new friends that day. Indeed my traveler friend found me immediately amongst the swarms of other travelers. In fact, she talked fondly about that airport meeting for years afterwards.

Sometimes I get tired of traveling because I'm in airplanes and hotels and I am on my own, I am alone. I am a very social person, so my husband says one day, "Why don't you bring something fun with you, do something fun when you are on the road?"

We have a darling bean bag frog that sits on our bed. He approaches me one day when I'd just finished packing and said, "Take Froggy on the road!"

"I don't know about that. I don't really have room for the frog."

"Put her here!"

He puts the frog into my bag so that's its vivacious little face sticks out of the top.

I said, "I'm not walking around with the frog sticking out of my bag."

"Too late!" he says as he loads my bags into the car for the airport.

And it was a hit. Everybody loved me and my frog. I went through airport security and all the security people said, "Look at the frog!" I had to hang out in security for an extra 15 minutes until they had all written down the brand name.

I get on the airplane and the flight attendant says, "Woman on aisle 17 with a frog, take a look." I peak Froggy out in the aisle to wave at everyone. People in the elevators and the cab drivers all wanted to chat about my frog. It was like I brought a puppy with me.

It's strange. You do these things and all of a sudden people aren't strangers anymore, you're having fun interactions and those little moments that you think don't make a difference in people's lives are a little drop in the bucket, that bring joy to you and others.

Goodness knows there is enough suffering in this world; it actually doesn't take much to balance it out with a little joy.

# Chapter 8
## Types of Humor to Use at Work

*Life was meant to be lived as play.* - Plato

I often ask a live audience to raise their hand if they consider themselves as having a good sense of humor. How would you answer that question? If the majority of the people in the room are in a people-oriented profession such as teaching, nursing, counseling or marketing most people raise their hand. On one occasion, however, I was speaking to a room that consisted entirely of tax auditors. When I asked the same question, what do you think happened? Almost everyone puts their hand up as well. I was surprised.

There were two administrative assistants sitting up front. One turns to the other and says, "Look over there, Frank put his hand up. He can't be funny. He works in fraud detection!"

On the break, I talk to Frank. I say, "I noticed you raise your hand about having a sense of humor. Do you think people at work or your clients see you this way?"

"No! Not at all. I HAVE to be *scary Frank--the audit guy*," he says with a big grin on his face.

I nod.

In a whisper, he adds, "But, I'm in a comedy troupe on the weekends."

"Really? And no one at work knows this about you?"

He shakes his head.

"That's quite a big part of your personality you are leaving behind on the weekends. What about including that more in your workday?"

"I can't make fun of people getting audited!"

"You don't have to make fun OF people, you could have fun WITH people."

I gave him some ideas and he e-mailed me back a few weeks later with an amazing story, which I will tell you about in a moment.

There are two myths about humor at work. The first one is that you need to be a kind of standup comedian to even label yourself as having a sense of humor. If you can laugh at life and yourself, you have a good sense of humor. Apparently less than 1% of the population actually doesn't have that part of their brain. Laughter comes bundled with your bio computer hard drive, as I like to say. Some people just use it more than others. What you focus on grows. If you'd like to build your sense of humor, just focus on it more often. There are huge rewards in doing so. One of the first things that helps is to just label yourself as having a good sense of humor. Give yourself permission to be playful. Many people grew up in an environment, like I did, where humor, laughter and playfulness were ignored at best and invalidated at worst. Sometimes you just need to change the programming in your head and it all comes back again.

The second myth is that you should avoid humor at work because someone will get offended. "Put down" humor is only one of 1000 ways of creating laughter at work. It's generally best to avoid teasing, sarcasm and ridicule at work unless there is already a positive relationship between two people, and that is an established way of interacting. Avoid "put down" humor with strangers or people you don't know very well. They might take it the wrong way. The best and easiest kind of humor to use at work is playful, spontaneous interactions, where you are laughing WITH people and not AT she them.

In fact, Peter J. McLachlan, in his book *Mentally Tough* talks about **Emotional Tones of Humor**. Humor is an element like fire. You can use it to build warmth and excitement, to shed light on an issue and to "cook" things up. At the same time, you can use it to deflate, annoy or destroy. Be aware of your intention and the outcome you want. This list below can help you become aware of the mood or energy level of others by the type of humor they are using.

1. **Despairing Humor** = Low-energy and Negative Tone:
- Laughing at the misery of life
- Black Humor
- Sick Jokes
- Self-Deprecating
- Twisted/Weird

Movie or TV show example: *Fargo*

Joke Example: *I'd like to die like my grandfather who died in his sleep -- unlike the six other screaming passengers in his car.*

2. **Aggressive Humor** = High-energy and Negative Tone:

- Laughing at the expense of others
- Teasing
- Sarcasm
- Ridicule
- Practical Jokes
- Humor That Reinforces Stereotypes
- Humor That Exposes an Uncomfortable Truth

Movie or TV show example: *Fargo*

Joke Example: *I'd like to die like my grandfather who died in his sleep -- unlike the six other screaming passengers in his car.*

3. **Silly Humor** = Low-energy and Positive Tone:

- Giggling at anything
- Simple Puns and Riddles
- Groaners
- Farce
- Exaggeration

Movie or TV show example: *Dumb & Dumber*

Joke Example: *How do you know elephants are in your fridge? The door won't close.*

4. **Insightful Humor** = High-energy and Positive Tone:

- Laughing with People
- Complex Forms of Playfulness
- Sophisticated Puns and Riddles
- Observational Humor That Opens Minds
- Laughing at Universal Human Truths

Movie or TV show example: *Groundhog's Day*

Joke Example: *Life is like photography. We use the negatives to develop.*

You can also use these tones of humor to create a different mood and energy level, to expose truth, to rapport build. If you are working with the group that uses *Despairing Humor* a lot, like police officers and emergency room personnel, you may need to start there in order to build rapport. If you need to expose the truth in a more indirect way, you might find using *Aggressive Humor* to be a better approach. If you are working with children or group that is in a positive mood but low-energy, you might need to use *Silly Humor*. If you want to increase energy and set a more positive tone, steer towards *Insightful Humor*. No type of humor is better than any other, it just all depends on what kind of result you want.

Let's get back to Frank's story. He e-mailed me that a few weeks later he was auditing the company. He was sitting in the back room with all the receipts and people were *icing* him, ignoring him. He was used to that. At one point, he goes out to the water cooler and people are talking about American politics. At the time, George Bush was in power, so he did his George W. Bush impression in response to one of their comments. They look over at him. One of them says, "That was pretty good. Who else can you do? "He started doing his Al Pacino impression and his Michael Jackson moonwalk. People gathered around laughing and then after a few minutes everyone went back to their office. About 15 minutes later, he said that the receptionist brought him a special box of chocolate. He said, "That kind of thing never happens when I'm doing an audit." On the weekend, a couple of them came to his show. When he was finished the audit he had to give the company a fine, but several people still hugged him when he left. They were sad to see him go. After that, he started bringing his playful personality much more to his job. I love that story because it illustrates something important. Even if we don't like the job, or it's boring, or mind-numbing, humor is what connects us at the heart. It reminds us that we are all humans doing these jobs together and that's what makes the process of doing it all so much better and more enjoyable.

# Chapter 9
## Fun at Work Ideas

*Love may make the world go around, but it's laughter that keeps us from getting dizzy. – Donald Zochert*

Planning on-going celebrations and fun at work is an excellent way to enhance creativity and reward people. It can build the social bonds that help groups make it through the tough times. Most of the ideas below come from a survey of the most popular ideas used at medium to large organizations in North America. Most of these ideas cost little or nothing and require virtually no time beyond informing people about what's happening. You can weave these ideas into your workday or use them to plan a special event.

**A. Special Event Days:**

1. **Hallowe'en**: apple bobbing, pumpkin carving, wear scary costume, pumpkin pie eating contest, make your own mask out of disposable workplace items (ie. paper clips, etc.)
2. **Oktoberfest**: polka music, tuba & accordion players, best sauerkraut contest, wear Lederhosen and Birkenstocks
3. **Caribbean Day**: limbo contest, kettle drums, rubber tropical fish in the water cooler, have a dance teacher show everyone the Electric Slide.
4. **Christmas/Hanukkah/end of the year**: play the recycled gift game, Elf costume contest, buy and wrap gifts for the homeless.
5. **Valentine's Day**: wear red or pink, all chip in money for the Heart Foundation, send a Valentine to someone who most needs it, play old Sinatra love songs all day
6. **St. Patrick's Day**: wear green, spray hair green, put a

pot of gold (chocolates) under someone's desk, dress up as a leprechaun

7. **Don't Laugh Day**: Any time someone laughs they have to put money in a basket that then gets given to charity at the end of the day. People often laugh more on this day than any other day of the year.

8. **Back to School**: Dress like you did in Grade 7, give out action hero lunch boxes, jive or disco contest, hula hoop contest

9. **New Years Eve**: come as your favourite New Year's resolution.

## B. Theme Days with clothes:

1. Wild hats
2. odd socks
3. Fun underwear
4. Tacky tourist
5. Tacky ties
6. Clashing clothes
7. Casual dress

## C. Contests:

Try these at lunchtime or at social events:

**Balloon shaving** - Put shaving cream on helium balloons and see who can shave off the cream without bursting the balloon.

**Lip synch** - Learn a piece of mucis very well. Play the music and synch your lips to the sound of the singer without actually singing. Have several people in the competition. w

**Air band** (or air orchestra) - Put on music that you know well. With a group of people mime the various instruments. Have teams and judge which group is the winner.

**Two Truths & One Lie**: Everyone tells three facts about themselves, one of which is lie. Others try to guess which is the lie.

**Baby Pictures** - Ask people to bring in photos of themselves as a baby. The younger, the better. Put them on a bulletin board and guess who is who.

**Pet Pictures** - Ask people to bring in photos of one of their pets. Put them on a bulletin board and guess which pet belongs to which person.

**Worst Hair Day** - Everyone shows up to a group gathering with "bad hair" and one person is the winner.

**Caption Contest** - Put up a cartoon without a caption. Get people to make up a new caption that fits the cartoon.

**Giant bubbles** - Get plastic tubs full of bubble soap and get the giant bubble makers from the toy store. Give out a prize for the first person to make the biggest bubble.

**Decorated elbows, hands or feet** - Get body paint and draw faces on elbows, hands or feet. Give prizes for the best ones.

**Golf course** - Put out paper cups, balls and golf clubs. Create a golf course through the office or meeting area. On breaks people try to get a whole in one.

**Clean joke-a-day challenge** - The department where most people participate wins.

**Snowman building** - An the lunch break put people into teams and go to a local park area.

**Best paper airplane** - As a fun break during a meeting.

**Excuses** - Put up a sheet of paper and ask people to contribute the best excuse they've ever heard or given for: being late, returning merchandise, not paying their bill, etc. (use a real one, or make one up)

**Treasure Hunt**: Give out five clues (one each day) and publish them in newsletter. Have them give progressive information to point participants to the location of a prize.

17. **Examples of prizes**:
    - Special food or drink in the cafeteria named after you
    - Your own parking space
    - Book, poster, coffee mug, or T-shirt
    - Ask for prize donations from boss, co-workers, or business services that your organization uses

**D. Awards Night:**

Each person gets given the name of someone else at work. They choose an award title and a fitting prize to go with it. Choose upbeat, non put-down prizes. Here are some examples of titles and awards:

- Best blow-dried hair…can of salon mousse.
- Perkiest phone voice…phone neck rest.
- Most good-natured morning person…fresh coffee
- Best manicured nails…hot pink nail polish.
- Most legible handwriting…Mickey Mouse pen.

**E. On-Going Activities:**

1. **What's Good?** Begin meetings by asking each person "What's going good in your dept?"
2. **Joy Break Box**: fill it with fun things such as nerf frisbees, deck of cards, noses, costumes, cartoon books, humor books, songbooks, etc.
3. **Stroll Meetings:** For 2-3 person meetings, go on a walk together in nature (bring a mini recorder to capture ideas and decisions for the minutes).
4. **Game Break**: co-workers get together for 15 min. over lunch to play cards, frisbee, word game, teambuilding game, board game, etc. (assign key person to organize it).
5. **Humor bulletin board**: Place in a high traffic area. Post funny articles, cartoons, staff photos, quotes, jokes, etc.

6. **Best Mistakes Stories**: allot 5 minutes during meetings for people to share any recent embarrassing or funny stories from their work or personal life.
7. **Mural**: Put up a large piece of paper in a common area. Pick a theme and ask people to contribute to it over a period of time. They can draw pictures, doodles, write words, poetry, paste magazine clippings, etc.
8. **Lunchtime Fun**: Go out to lunch with co-workers all wearing noses or fun hats. Give an outrageously good tip to the waiter. Sing the waiter a song for doing such a good job.
9. **Ask for Acknowledgment**: when you've had a tough day, or you finally finished a project -- ask for a standing ovation from co-workers.
10. **Chair Massage Day**: Invite a practitioner to come in give everyone a 15 min. chair massage during the day.
11. **Friday Flower Day**: Each Friday one person brings in a bouquet and gives it away with a note of acknowledgment to someone at work. The next Friday that person brings in a new bouquet for another person.
12. **Lapel Buttons**: Decorate yourself by wearing pins or buttons with funny messages. For a meeting which promises to be stress-filled, try a button that reads, "Save time...see it my way!"

### F. Unusual Reasons to Celebrate:

- **Unbirthdays** (pick anyone and give them a surprise birthday party)
- **Decorate the boss's office** with streamers, flowers and balloons
- **International Fun at Work Day** is Feb. 27
- **New employee's first day on the job**
- **Santa shows up with gifts in July**
- **Nut Day in Belgium** (Dec. 15)

## G. Angel & Earthling:

- People write out their names, birthdays, favourite sport, colour, snack, etc., & anonymously exchange papers
- Each person then becomes an Angel to the person whose name they receive.
- As an Angel you anonymously surprise your Earthling with acknowledgments, gifts, and special favours.
- At a predetermined time (e.g. 3 months) Angels reveal their identities

# Chapter 10
## 6 Mistakes to Avoid - Using Fun at Work

1. **Not paying attention to intention.** Some people use fun and humor to covertly express anger. Be aware of your intention and the outcome you want beforehand. Look for inspiring ice-breakers rather than deflating ice-makers. Tip: when using "put down" humor focus on universal themes that all people can relate to rather than targeting certain groups or individuals.

2. **Starting with something too complicated or risky.** For example, don't start with the "Dress Like You Did in Grade 7" Day unless that kind of high play is the norm in your working environment. Start small and simple like putting up a bulletin board for cartoons, or beginning a client meeting with the question "What's Good?".

3. **Giving no prior warning or purpose for fun activities.** If people don't understand the benefits they may resist you. Give prior warning and educate people not only on the benefits but also how to do it successfully. Post an article on the bulletin board (like one of Carla's!), or bring in a speaker on the subject (like Carla!) - for those who didn't attend this one.

4. **Giving a mixed message.** Some organizations give lip service to fun at work, but the boss either won't join in or worse – reacts negatively when people risk new behavior. If you are the boss you need to role model fun at work or at least join in. Also, make it clear there will be no negative consequences for trying new ideas. Troubleshoot ideas that don't fly (see #6).

**5. Delegating to a cynic.** Some people will need to devote time to organize and implement ideas. Don't choose people who are doubtful of the benefits or reluctant to try new things. Choose people who are already good at practicing constructive fun at work or who are at least enthusiastic about trying. Assign them a role such as the "Director of Creativity" or have a committee called "The Fun Task Force".

**6. Giving up too quickly.** If a creative idea doesn't fly, don't decide that all ideas won't work. Instead, debrief it with your staff and clients to find out why it didn't work, and try another approach. For example, a call center tried playing Top 40 hits to keep their Saturday night shift more motivated (who were mostly university students). Some students loved it and some complained. The complainers said they preferred silence because they were trying to study between calls. Instead of dropping the idea, they created a separate room for those who wanted silence.

# Chapter 11
## Discover Your D.A.N.C.E. Humor Personality Style

I have often heard people say they have no sense of humor because they cannot tell jokes. Telling jokes is only one of a hundred different ways to elicit laughter from people. Each person has a different style of humor. The trick is to find your style and build on your innate strengths.

For example, are you the kind of person who can keep people riveted while telling a story about your latest trip to the grocery store, yet always blow the timing on a joke? Perhaps you like to clown around being playful, but get lost trying to do witty one-liners?

Take the self-quiz on the next few pages to find out your dominant style. These humor styles are, of course, highly generalized. Most people have qualities of more than one style, or will tend to switch from one style to the other depending on their environment. Use this information as a place to start. If you begin with humor that suits your personality style, you will have more success than if you try something too foreign right from the start.

Once you experience success in your dominant style, you can expand your skills to include different types of humor to appeal to different types of people. That is why I have included a fifth style that includes and transcends all the other styles. It is the most creative and versatile style and therefore is labeled **The Expert.**

# Take the Quiz

1. At a large social gathering, you are most likely to

   a. interact with many different people, including strangers.
   b. talk one-on-one mostly with familiar faces.
   c. use the opportunity to make important connections with key people.
   d. leave as soon as possible.

2. When you first arrive at a meeting you are usually

   a. a bit late, and try to sneak in the back without being noticed.
   b. purposely a bit late; you like to get there when things have really started happening.
   c. arrive right on time and feel impatient if the meeting starts late.
   d. arrive early so that you can be ready and organized when the meeting starts.

3. If you were famous, which career would most suit you?

    a. Movie star
    b. Head of your own successful company
    c. Inventor
    d. Humanitarian

4. What style of comedy do you most enjoy watching?

    a. Something warm and friendly
    b. Clever and witty
    c. Assertive, satirical, or pointed humor
    d. Wacky, farcical or a spoof

5. Of these four personality traits, which do you consider to be your strongest?

a. Compassionate
b. Assertive
c. Imaginative
d. Persistent

6. The statement that most closely describes you is

a. sensible and frugal.
b. rational and quick-witted.
c. sensitive and reliable.
d. creative and fiery.

7. Which appeals to you the most?

a. Taking action on a calculated risk.
b. Creating harmonious human relationships.
c. Discovering the secret behind a complex mystery.
d. Going to an exciting social event.

8. Which rules you more?

a. Your heart
b. Your head
c. Your wallet
d. Your libido

9. New and non-routine interaction with others

a. usually stimulates and energizes you.
b. revitalizes you, if you have a special connection with someone in the process.

c. taxes your reserves, and you aren't afraid to let people know it.
d. taxes your reserves, so you quietly slip away when no one is watching.

10. When doing group projects, which part of the process is most important to you?

a. Creating relationships with people
b. Sorting out who is playing what role in the project
c. Organizing the way the project is done
d. Making sure the process of doing it is fun and exciting

11. If you suddenly have some spare time on a weekend, what you usually most want to do is

a. contact several friends and see if there is something fun going on.
b. have some quality time with one or just a few people.
c. do competitive sports such as golf, tennis, or soccer.
d. find your own space and focus your energy on one specific hobby.

12. You want to buy a special gift for a new friend that you don't know very well. You are most likely to

a. buy the first thing you see that you intuitively think they would like.
b. carefully find just the right thing, after much comparison shopping.
c. buy the same special gift you always buy for special people.
d. get someone else to buy the gift, or just give your friend money.

13. Which description most fits you?

a. Hard-working and ambitious
b. Animated and gregarious
c. Focused and efficient
d. Cooperative and gentle

14. Most of the time, when working, you prefer

a. to do your job in your own way in your own time.
b. to be part of a team working together.
c. to be the inspirational leader of that team.
d. to work on your own and delegate tasks to others on your team.

15. When the phone rings you

a. answer it immediately and talk at length.
b. look forward to the call, but wait a few rings before answering.
c. deal with whoever it is quickly and efficiently.
d. hope someone else will answer it or screen the call.

16. Your favorite type of clothing to wear when attending a celebratory event is

a. comfortable and low-key – I don't put much time into clothing choice.
b. unique and creative – I like to stand out.
c. formal and classy – I take time to look my absolute best.
d. what most everyone else is wearing – I want to fit in.

17. Which genre of fiction/movie/TV do you most prefer?

a. Mystery or science fiction (e.g., *Sherlock Holmes, Star Wars*)
b. Feel-good story or romantic comedy (e.g., *This is Us, Bridget Jones Diary*)
c. Epic, adventure, or action (e.g., *Gladiator* or *The Bourne Identity, King Kong*)
d. Spoof/satire (e.g., *Best in Show* or *Austin Powers*)

18. Which is more admirable?

a. The ability to organize and be methodical
b. The ability to take charge in a chaotic situation
c. The ability to motivate others to succeed
d. The ability to be cooperative and collaborative

19. In terms of speakers/educators, you most respond to someone who can…

a. tell a good story.
b. shake up your perspective and challenge you.
c. demonstrate what they want you to learn or understand.
d. provide proof to back up their claims.

20. If someone challenges your opinion, your initial response is to

a. defend your perspective and keep going on the topic.
b . listen to their point of view and let it influence you.
c. neutrally acknowledge the comment and quickly change the topic.
d. get into a colorful debate until it resolves.

## The D.A.N.C.E. Humor Style Quiz - Answers

Circle the answers you chose. Then, add up the number of D's, A's, N's, and C's you have.

| | | | | |
|---|---|---|---|---|
| 1. | a. D | b. N | c. A | d. C |
| 2. | a. N | b. D | c. A | d. C |
| 3. | a. D | b. A | c. C | d. N |
| 4. | a. N | b. C | c. A | d. D |
| 5. | a. N | b. A | c. D | d. C |
| 6. | a. C | b. A | c. N | d. D |
| 7. | a. A | b. N | c. C | d. D |
| 8. | a. N | b. C | c. A | d. D |
| 9. | a. D | b. N | c. A | d. C |
| 10. | a. N | b. A | c. C | d. D |
| 11. | a. D | b. N | c. A | d. C |
| 12. | a. D | b. N | c. C | d. A |
| 13. | a. A | b. D | c. C | d. N |
| 14. | a. C | b. N | c. D | d. A |
| 15. | a. D | b. N | c. A | d. C |
| 16. | a. C | b. D | c. A | d. N |
| 17. | a. C | b. N | c. A | d. D |
| 18. | a. C | b. A | c. D | d. N |
| 19. | a. N | b. A | c. D | d. C |
| 20. | a. A | b. N | c. C | d. D |

Total D's \_\_\_\_ Total A's \_\_\_\_ Total N's \_\_\_\_ Total C's \_\_\_\_

**Scoring** Total should come to 20

1. D = Demonstrator
2. A = Assertor
3. N = Narrator
4. C = Contemplator.
5. E = Expert - If you scored evenly across the board

Read the next few pages on the five different D.A.N.C.E. humor styles. You will also see examples of famous comedians and one-liners from that style. Then think about others you interact with, and see if you can recognize their style. If you do presentations either one-to-one or to groups, see how you can match your style with your listener's style, increasing the chances of creating much more laughter.

### Demonstrator

Demonstrators are people oriented, fast paced, and enthusiastic. They usually have open body language and are animated and outgoing. They tend to prefer an informal atmosphere and enjoy socializing frequently. Demonstrators can be outrageous, spontaneous, and excitable. They are idea people who like to be in the limelight. Weaknesses of this type are that they can be unreliable, self-centered, overly optimistic and boundriless.

Many people drawn into traditional comedy performing are Demonstrators or have had to develop this kind of humor persona. In the TV Show *Big Bang Theory*, the character of Howard (Simon Helberg) is a Demonstrator with his high energy, outrageous comments and crazy colored clothes. Also, in the TV show *Modern Family*, Gloria (Sofia Vergara) is a Demonstrator with her big presence, loud voice and eye catching outfits. Late Night comics Conan O'Brien and Jimmy Fallon are both Demonstrators. Also, Steve Martin is a Demonstrator comedian. You can see his extraordinary talent for physical comedy and wacky characters in such movies as *The Jerk*, *Dirty Rotten Scoundrels*, and *All of Me*. For those who can remember, Buster Keaton, The Three Stooges, Gracie Allen, and Jerry Lewis were all Demonstrators. Their wild physical antics made them the top comedians of their day. Other famous comedians through the ages with this style are Lucille Ball, Wayne Brady from *Whose Line is it Anyway?*, and Carrot Top. Cartoonists such as Chuck Jones (*Looney Tunes*) or Friz Freleng (*The Pink Panther*) use a Demonstrator style as well.

## Humor Strengths

- Improvised humor
- Characters
- Impressions
- Using costumes, props, or magic
- Clowning
- Games
- Physical exaggeration
- Accents
- Farce

## Demonstrator Jokes

Demonstrator jokes usually include something off-the-wall or outrageous, and the topic is more often about people rather than concepts or things. Many impressionists, game show hosts, and character actors are Demonstrators. Their job throughout history has been to step outside the norm, exaggerate the situation or take the mundane into the absurd so that we stop taking life so seriously.

## Here are samples of Demonstrators jokes:

"How many surrealist painters does it take to screw in a light bulb? Three. One to change the bulb, one to hold the giraffe, and one to fill the bathtub with multicolored dental instruments."
    - Mitchell Yawitz

*"If you want to be safe on the streets at night, carry a projector and slides of your last vacation."*
    - Helen Mundis

"Good thing I was born a woman, or I'd have been a drag queen."
	- Dolly Parton

"I handed in a script last year and the studio didn't change one word. The word they didn't change was on page 87." – Steve Martin

"My report card always said, 'Jim finishes first and then disrupts the other students."
	- Jim Carrey

"Whenever I have to choose between two evils, I always like to try the one I haven't tried before."
	- Mae West

"The Russians love Brooke Shields because her eyebrows remind them of Leonid Brezhnev."
	- Robin Williams

"When my mother had to get dinner for eight she'd just make enough for sixteen and only serve half."
	- Gracie Allen

## Assertor

Assertors are fast paced and direct like Demonstrators, but tend to be more task oriented. They are hard working, ambitious leader types who are good at making decisions quickly and efficiently. They are goal oriented, assertive, and confident. Assertors are the take-charge people who let nothing stop them. Their weaknesses include being too impatient, competitive, and judgmental.

In the TV Show *Big Bang Theory*, the character of Bernadette (Melissa Rauch) is an Assertor with her strong opinions and forthright manner. Also, in the TV show *Modern Family*, Jay (Ed O'Neill) is an Assertor with his Alpha male personality and assertive style of dealing with people. Entertainers such as Louis C.K., Chris Rock, Julia Louis-Dreyfus, Sharon Horgan, and Bill Maher and Rita Rudner are all Assertors. Late Night Satirists such as Stephen Colbert *and* David Letterman are also both Assertors. Also, maybe you can remember back to the comedy of Dennis Miller, Joan Rivers, George Carlin, and Don Rickles? Many comedy duos often consist of an Assertor and a Demonstrator, such as George Burns and Gracie Allen, Dean Martin and Jerry Lewis, Stan Laurel and Oliver Hardy, or Bud Abbott and Lou Costello, respectively. Cartoonists such as Jim Davis (*Garfield*), Garry Trudeau (*Doonesbury*), or Bill Watterson (*Calvin and Hobbes*) use an Assertor style in their comic strips.

## Humor Strengths

- Stand-up comedy
- Roasts
- Political satire
- Humor that uncovers hidden truths
- Jokes
- One-liners
- Pointed observations

## Assertor Jokes

Assertor jokes usually have an edge, point out an uncomfortable truth, or include an aspect of power balancing. Many late-night comedians are like the king's court jesters of the olden days. Their job is to poke fun at authority figures when they get out of balance.

"How many honest politicians does it take to screw in a light bulb? Both of them."
	- Anonymous

"Based on what you know about him in history books, what do you think Abraham Lincoln would be doing if he were alive today?
	1. Writing his memoirs of the Civil War.
	2. Advising the President.
	3. Desperately clawing at the inside of his coffin."
	-David Letterman

"Whenever I date a guy, I think, is this the man I want my children to spend their weekends with?"
	- Rita Rudner

"I'm going to write a book about the South. I'm going to call it 'When Beautiful Places Happen to Bad People.'"
	- Brett Butler

"The day I worry about cleaning my house, is the day Sears comes out with a riding vacuum cleaner."   - Roseanne Barr

"If you think nobody cares about you, try missing a couple of payments."
    - Anonymous

"If a woman has to choose between catching a fly ball and saving an infant's life, she will choose to save the infant's life without even considering if there is a man on base."
    - Dave Barry

"Democracy is a form of government that substitutes election by the incompetent many for appointment by the corrupt few."
    - George Bernard Shaw

"A great many people think they are thinking when they are merely rearranging their prejudices."
    - William James

## Contemplator

Contemplators are task oriented like Assertors, however, they are more indirect and methodical. Contemplators tend to be analytical, detail-oriented thinker types. They are persistent, good problem solvers, and, they pride themselves on their orderliness and accuracy. Often seen alone, they tend to have quiet, low-key personalities. Their weaknesses include being too withdrawn, rigid, closed-minded, and overly pessimistic.

In the TV Show *Big Bang Theory*, the character of Sheldon (Jim Parsons) is a Contemplator with his mellow but highly intellectual quirkiness. Also, in the TV show *Modern Family*, Mitchell (Jesse Tyler Ferguson) is a Contemplator with his quieter personality and intellectual and fastidious of dealing with things. Entertainers who access the Contemplator style are often in the comedy-writing department rather than on stage. However, actors like Rick Moranis, Bob Newhart, and Woody Allen personify the quiet, intellectual style of Contemplators. Stand-up comics such as Steven Wright, Ellen Degeneris, and Paula Poundstone can enter into that dry, observational style, as well. Many of the top cartoonists such as Gary Larson (*The Far Side*) or Charles Schulz (*Peanuts*), are Contemplators. They enjoy the intellectual challenge and quiet life of a syndicated cartoonist.

### Humor Strengths

- Puns
- Wordplays
- Riddles
- Observational humor
- Intellectual humor
- Philosophical humor

## Contemplator Jokes

Contemplator jokes may include self-deprecating humor, black humor, wordplays, or wry observations. The topic is more often about concepts than about people. The Contemplator's job throughout history has been to look at the world from unusual angles and provide us with new perspectives. Here are some Contemplator jokes:

"How many programmers does it take to change a light bulb? None, that's hardware."
    -Anonymous

"It's not that I'm afraid to die, I just don't want to be there when it happens."
    - Woody Allen

"Whenever I think of the past it just brings back so many memories."
    - Steven Wright

"I used to work at the International House of Pancakes. It was a dream, and I made it happen."
    - Paula Poundstone

"Sorry, but my karma just ran over your dogma."
    - Swami Beyondananda

"Don't spend two dollars to dry clean a shirt. Donate it to the Salvation Army instead. They'll clean it and put it on a hanger. Next morning buy it back for seventy-five cents."
    - William Coronel

"Sometimes I lie awake at night, and I ask, 'Where have I gone wrong? Then a voice says to me, 'This is going to take more than one night.'"
    - Charlie Brown, *Peanuts* [Charles Schulz]

"I am not a vegetarian because I love animals; I am a vegetarian because I hate plants."
    - A. Whitney Brown

"My grandmother started walking five miles a day when she was sixty. She's ninety-seven now, and we don't know where the hell she is."
    - Ellen DeGeneris

## Narrator

Narrators are mellow and reserved like Contemplators, but they are more people oriented like Demonstrators. They are warm, friendly, gentle, and cooperative. They value relationships over tasks. They are good at listening, have a sweet temperament, and tend to be open-minded. Most people find them to be loving and emotionally intuitive. Weaknesses of this type are their lack of assertiveness and their tendency to get sidetracked.

In the TV Show *Big Bang Theory*, the characters Amy (Mayim Bialik) and Stuart (Kevin Sussman) are both Narrators with their caring, mellow demeanors. Also, in the TV show *Modern Family*, Cameron (Eric Stonestreet) and Phil (Ty Burrell) are both Narrators with their overly sensitive personalities always looking for ways to creating loving connections with people.

Back in the day, sitcom stars such as Mary Tyler Moore and Sally Field were both warm, sweet natured Narrator comedians in their TV shows. The comedy duo of Wayne & Garth (Mike Meyers & Dana Carvey) featured a Demonstrator and Narrator respectively. The late Gilda Radner and John Candy were both Narrators. For years, Narrator Johnny Carson had his late-night show pitted against his exact opposite, Assertor, David Letterman. Similarly, for years a Narrator show like *Oprah* was pitted against the opposing Assertor style of a show like *Geraldo*. Several comedy duos are made up of a Narrator and a Contemplator, such as Helen Hunt and Paul Reiser in *Mad About You*; Cheech and Chong, and the Smothers Brothers. Woody Allen often teamed himself with a female Narrator comedian such as Diane Keaton or Mia Farrow.

Many family sitcoms have a Narrator style of comedy, such as *Friends* or *Modern Family*. Family movies and romantic comedies such as *Parenthood, L.A. Story,* or *When Harry Met Sally* focus on a Narrator style. Cartoonists such as Cathy Guisewite (*Cathy*), or Lynn Johnston (*For Better or For Worse*) also use a Narrator style of humor in their comic strips.

**Humor Strengths**

- Storytelling
- Cooperative games
- Humor about relationships
- Preplanned as opposed to spontaneous
- Roleplays
- Audience interaction

**Narrator Jokes**

Narrator jokes tend to be about relationships between people, or charming characteristics about people. The Narrator's job throughout history has been to use humor to bring people closer, to break the ice, and to help us build compassion for ourselves and others. Here are a sampling of Narrator jokes:

"How many grandmothers does it take to screw in a light bulb? Three. One to change the bulb, and two to reminisce about how nice the old one was."
    - Anonymous

"The major concerns of social activist Emily Litella (Gilda Radner):
1. Conservation of national racehorses
2. Violins in schools
3. Soviet jewelry
4. Endangered feces"

"You know you're getting old when you stoop to tie your shoes and wonder what else you can do while you're down there."
    - George Burns

"Women definitely go to maintenance extremes. It's amazing the way women take care of all the hair on their bodies. One of the great mysteries to me is the fact that a woman could pour hot wax on her legs, rip the hair out by the roots, and still be afraid of a spider."
    - Jerry Seinfeld

"In response to the recent earthquake 'The God is Dead' meeting that was scheduled for tonight, has been cancelled.
    - Johnny Carson

"If dogs could talk it would take a lot of the fun out of owning one."
    - Andy Rooney

## One Joke/ Four Styles

Here is a joke to better help you understand the four styles:

Four nobles in Medieval times who each embodied a different humor style were sentenced to execution. The executioner pulled the rope, and the blade came down only to stop inches before their necks. The Sheriff of the town decided it was a sign from God that they were innocent and so set them all free.

The Assertor announced, "I told you I was innocent!"
The Demonstrator called out, "Let's party!"
The Narrator went up to the executioner, hugged him and said, "I just want you to know I don't take this personally."
The Contemplator said, "I think I see the problem."

## Expert

Experts are the fifth type of humorist, and typically they can access most styles of humor. If your Humor Style Quiz score came out fairly even across the board, consider yourself an Expert, or on your way there. To some extent, we are all a hybrid of many styles. The more balanced we can become, the more tools we have in our toolkit, the better prepared we are for the humor challenges we may encounter in life.

Experts can be both people oriented and task oriented. They can flip between a slow-paced style and a fast-paced one often with great comic effect. They are open at certain times when it feels appropriate and reserved when that feels best. When the situation calls for it, they will be direct in their communication. When a more indirect approach serves, they will opt for this route. They tend to stay in the present moment, and utilize whatever tools seem best for the occasion. They can be great writers of comedy as well as great performers. They both plan their humor carefully, and break free into spontaneity when necessary. Their style is congruent with the situation. Their position is one of wholeness and free movement in any direction. All parts of themselves are in balance. A weakness of this type is that they can challenge the status quo too much, causing others to feel off-balance or uncomfortable.

Comedians who are versatile actors in many areas are often Experts, such as the late, Robin Williams, and Jim Carrey, Lily Tomlin, Emma Thompson, Peter Sellers, Whoopi Goldberg, Will Ferrell, Tom Hanks, Steve Carell, Bill Murray Peter Sellers, Billy Crystal and Kristen Wiig. They have ventured into such varied areas as stand-up, improv, sketch comedy, dramatic roles, movie acting, TV roles, writing, and directing. There are many behind-the-scenes humorists who are Experts.

They are producing, directing and writing, often being the innovators of new projects. Some Experts such as Charlie Chaplin, Spalding Gray, Alan Alda, Albert Brooks, Goldie Hawn, Rob Reiner, Ron Howard, Mike Nichols and Elaine May were able to be behind the scenes and also perform.

Experts move past stereotypes, conventions, and styles to pioneer something new. According to most comedians, an audience of comedians is the toughest. They can see behind the comedian's bag of tricks and are usually analyzing the performer rather than surrendering to the comic experience. In his book *The Republic*, the ancient Greek scholar Plato referred to the philosopher-king as the ideal ruler because of his pioneering innovation.

Hal Erickson, a comedy reviewer, said that Albert Brooks was this "comedian-philosopher-king of whom Plato spoke" because of his innovative style. Brooks is one of the few comedians who can make other comics laugh.

## Humor Strengths

- Humor with a general appeal
- High concept and involvement
- Mind-expanding concepts
- Characters with depth
- Performance storytelling
- Creating new comic formats

## Expert Jokes

Expert jokes use humor to philosophize and to poke fun at human foibles rather than at specific people. They also use humor as a vehicle for creativity. Experts are likely to create new kinds of jokes, physicalizations, observations, and unusual forms of delivery. They may choose to demonstrate humor one moment then cut to the truth, move into narrative, and end with a contemplative style. They find a synthesis between many kinds of humor, either putting them together in new ways, creating a hybrid, or transforming two styles into a completely new third style. Here are some Expert jokes:

*"How many Zen Masters does it take to screw in a light bulb? Two. One to screw in the bulb and one not to screw in the bulb."*
    - Anonymous

*"Reality is the leading cause of stress amongst those in touch with it. I can take it in small doses, but as a lifestyle I find it too confining."*
    - Lily Tomlin in her show The Search for Signs of Intelligent Life in the Universe
    (written by Jane Wagner)

"In the end, everything is a gag."
- Charlie Chaplin

"Not one shred of evidence supports the notion that life is serious."
– Plato

"Experience is that marvelous thing that enables you to recognize a mistake when you make it again."
- F. P. Jones

"*To err is human. To really screw up, you need a computer.*"
- Anonymous

# Chapter 12
## Reclaiming Your Birthright to Live a Joyful Life

Remember I was also going to tell you about another incident that had a huge impact on changing my personality? As I mentioned, I came from a humorously challenged family, but an ironic thing happened when my mother become terminally ill relatively young.

The notion that life is short became very real to her. And her entire personality changed. She said *let's have fun*. She moved out to the country. She started wearing brightly colored clothes and flowers in her hair. She went back to things she loved when she was young, like singing and dancing. I'd never seen my mother laugh – that big, hearty belly kind of laugh -- until she was very ill.

She really just let it all go. She didn't care if the cheque book was balanced. She didn't care that there were wrinkles in the tablecloth. She made joy a number one priority and didn't care if people thought she was weird for wearing wild clothes and singing out of tune. Near the end of her life she warned me not to go down the same road as her.

She said, "Remember that life is short, and you don't know when your last day will be. It could be tomorrow for all you know. Do you really want to be spending your last moments annoyed that you can't get through traffic more quickly?"

The hospice workers that were with her at the end told me that attitude shifts like that happen often near the end of life. When people talk about their regrets, they rarely say "I wish I'd owned a nicer car." They never say "I wish I'd raised profit share by 4% more." They usually wish they'd had more moments of joy, and fun, and really appreciated and loved more. In those last few months of her life, I made that promise to myself that I would lighten up, and took it a step further and decided to lighten up the world with my work as a speaker, trainer and author.

When I look at most old photos of my mother, she is almost never smiling. But, whenever I think of her now she is smiling. And so I can remember the person that she became at the end of her life.

My father was very serious, too. Strangely, I never knew anything about his past. My mother has told me many fascinating stories about her life, especially leading up to her death. It felt like an important handing down of memories, knowledge and wisdom. Perhaps it was a way for her to sort through her life and let regrets go, find forgiveness and better learn life's lessons before leaving this world.

When my father was near the end of his life, I pushed him to tell me stories. As usual, he replied that he didn't like to talk about his past. He said he had no photos and no mementos and that he had lost all that in the war in Europe.

Nevertheless, I got him a journal which was a list of questions. It's the kind of thing you give to elderly people to trigger memories about family, career, travels and various aspects of life. I gave it to him for Christmas and he politely thanked me and put it away in a drawer. I could tell he wasn't going to do it. I nagged him a few times until he completed the first page. Then I gave up. Four months later he died at the age of 81.

As I was going through all the things in his house, I found the book of questions and re-read the first page. I was about to store the book away, when I decided to just turn the page. I

soon realized he had written an answer to every single question. He was filling it out up until the last days of his life!

What I found out that he didn't want anybody to know is that his family was related to gypsies, on his mother's side. And his family owned a carnival. This was in middle Europe during the time of Nazi occupation, and gypsies were some of the first people sent to concentration camps. You didn't want *anyone* to know you were related to gypsies or Bohemians or Travelers as they were sometimes called.

Also, a family fun fair business was not considered very respectable in those days. It was fascinating to discover this, because it helped me understand at least one of the reasons why he didn't want to talk about his past.

That said, for me the idea of being related to gypsies seemed romantic and not something to hide. All of a sudden, my love of fun fairs, reading tarot cards and listening to *The Gypsy Kings* music made sense. Fun was there in my heritage all along.

The truth is, fun has been killed off several times throughout history but we are at a time now when we can reclaim the importance of fun, especially with our scientific knowledge of how important positive psychology is for our entire well-being.

Fun, laughter and play are at the core of our reasons for living. It's time we stopped trivializing it and instead, validate its importance in our everyday lives. May this short book inspire you to improve your *laugh life* one joyful step at a time.

# About Carla Rieger

Carla Rieger is the Director of Artistry of Change Productions Inc. She is an award-winning author, comedienne, speaker and presentation skills coach. She helps people create new possibilities and potentials through unleashing creative genius.

In addition to 23 years as a business communication and creativity expert, she has written five plays, two screenplays, hundreds of short stories and articles, three books, one novel and has been a solo show artist.

Her work has been featured on radio, TV and in magazines. She has presented to over 200,000 people internationally as a speaker, trainer, facilitator and performer.

For more information on how to:

- access **free online trainings and downloadable resources**
- join one of our **online courses**
- **book Carla Rieger as a speaker** for your event

...go to [http://carlarieger.com/](http://carlarieger.com/)

www.ingramcontent.com/pod-product-compliance
Lightning Source LLC
Chambersburg PA
CBHW070210230526
45471CB00002B/900

# Invisible Intelligence

# Smart Sensing Transforming Everyday Life

Taylor Royce

Copyright © 2024 Taylor Royce

All rights reserved.